The Joy of Folk Songs

The Joy Of Folk Songs is a tuneful anthology of favorite folk melodies. All categories of the American folk idiom are represented in very easy piano arrangements with words and chord names. Here are Love Ballads, Cowboy with Work Songs, Lullabies, Spirituals and a carefully chosen group of popular aires from other nations.

Within the past decade there has been a marked increase in the popularity of folk music in America. People who had never gotten closer to folklore than an occasional humming of "Home Sweet Home" are familiar with literally hundreds of original American aires. The entire field of present day music is folk orientated. This healthy trend has its effect on music education too. That is why we feel that The Joy Of Folk Songs is not only a source of entertainment for any piano player and a handy guide book for a song fest or sing-along, but it is also an ideally suitable companion book for the beginning piano student.

T0052964

Distributed throughout the world by Hal Leonard,
7777 West Bluemound Road, WI 53213Milwaukee
42 Wigmore Street Maryleborne WIU 2 RY, London
4 Lentara Court Cheltenham, Victoria, 9132 Australia

Contents

Blow The Man Down

Comfortably, with a swing

1. Come all you young fel - lows who fol - low the sea, To me
2. I'll sing you a song, a good song of the sea, To me

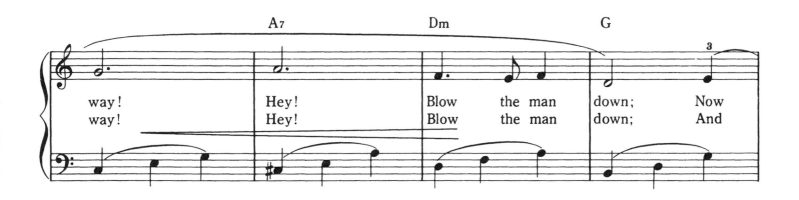

way!   Hey!   Blow the man down;   Now
way!   Hey!   Blow the man down;   And

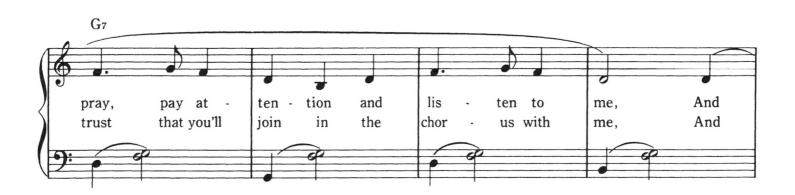

pray,   pay at - ten - tion and lis - ten to me,   And
trust   that you'll join in the chor - us with me,   And

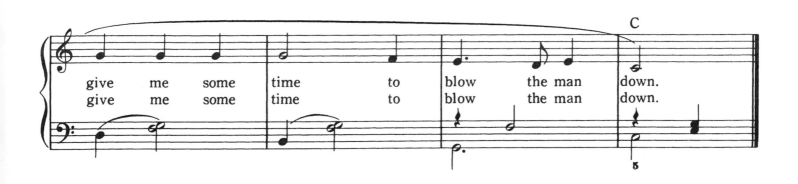

give me some time to blow the man down.
give me some time to blow the man down.

I'm Sad And I'm Lonely

2. I'll build me a cabin on the mountain so high,

Where the blackbirds can't find me or hear my sad cry.

Young ladies take warning, take warning from me:

Don't wast your affections on a young man so free.

The Railroad Corral

Lively, with a lilt

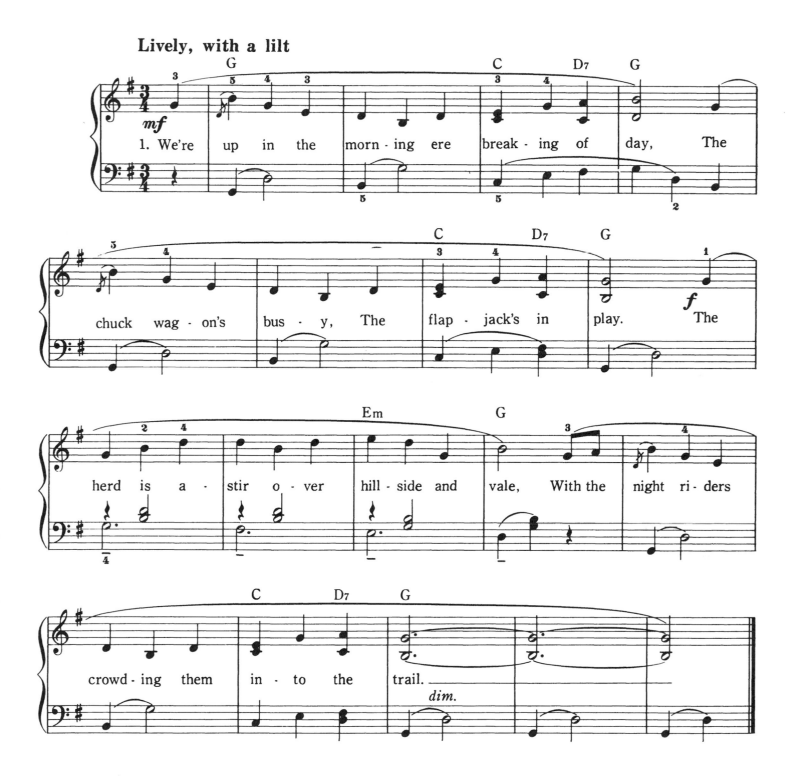

2. Come take up your cinches, come shake out your reins,

Come wake your old bronco and break for the plains;

Come roust out your steers from the long chaparral,

For the outfit is off to the railroad corral.

The Foggy, Foggy Dew

2. One night when she was kneeling so close
by my side,

When I was fast asleep,

And she threw her loving arms around my neck,

And she then began to weep.

She wept, she cried, she tore her hair,

Ah me! What could I do?

I had to do what's right, so I gave her my arms

To protect her from the foggy, foggy dew.

3. Again I'm a bach'lor, I live with my son,

We work at the weaver's trade.

And ev'ry time I look into his brown eyes,

I recall a fair young maid.

He reminds me of the winter - time

And of the summer too,

And the many, many times that I held her in
my arms,

Just to keep her from the foggy, foggy dew.

Black Is The Color Of My True Love's Hair

The Erie Canal

Moderately, with vigor

I've got a mule, her name is Sal, Fif-teen miles on the

E - rie Ca-nal.___ She's a good ol' work-er and a good ol' pal,

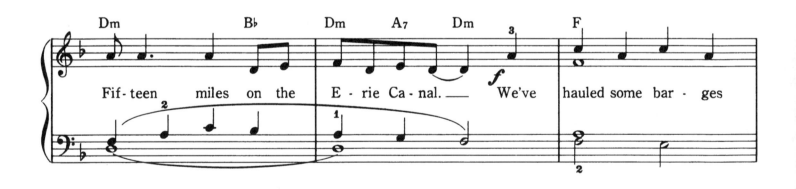

Fif-teen miles on the E - rie Ca-nal.___ We've hauled some bar - ges

in our day, Filled with lum-ber, coal and hay, And

2. We'd better look around for a job, old gal,
   Fifteen miles on the Erie Canal.
   'Cause you bet your life I'd never part with Sal,
   Fifteen miles on the Erie Canal.

   Get up there, mule, here comes a lock,
   We'll make Rome 'bout six o'clock,
   One more trip and back we'll go,
   Right back home to Buffalo.

   Chorus:

Deep River

Rock-a My Soul

Poor Boy

12

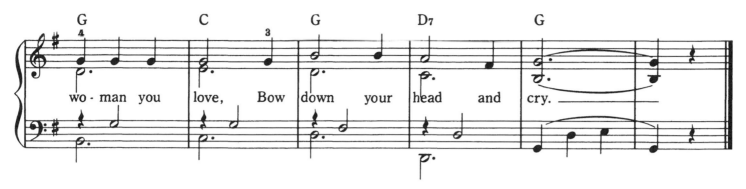

wo-man you love, Bow down your head and cry. ———

2. I followed her for months and months,
   She offered me her hand;
   We were just about to be married, when
   She ran off with a gamblin' man.   Chorus:

3. He came at me with a big jack-knife,
   I went for him with lead,
   And when the fight was over, poor boy,
   He lay down beside me dead.   Chorus:

4. They took me to the big jail-house,
   The months and months rolled by;
   The jury found me guilty, poor boy,
   And the judge said, "You must die." Chorus:

5. "Oh, do you bring me silver, poor boy,
   Or do you bring me gold?"
   "I bring you neither," said the man,
   "I bring you a hangman's fold." Chorus:

6. "Oh, do you bring me pardon, poor boy,
   To turn me a-loose?"
   "I bring you nothing," said the man,
   "Except a hangman's noose."   Chorus:

7. And yet they call this justice, poor boy,
   Then justice let it be !
   I only killed a man that was
   A-fixin' to kill me.   Chorus:

On Springfield Mountain

Moderately

1. On Spring-field moun-tain there did dwell A love-ly youth; I knew him well. Too
2. This love-ly youth one day did go Down to the mead-ow for to mow.

roo-de-nay, too-roo-de-noo, Too-roo-de-nay, too-roo-de-noo.

3. He scarce had mowed half round the field
   When a p'izen sarpent bit his heel. Chorus:

4. They took hime home to Molly dear,
   Which made him feel so very queer. Chorus:

5. Now Molly had two ruby lips
   With which the p'izen she did sip. Chorus:

6. Now Molly had a rotting tooth
   And so the p'izen killed them both. Chorus:

Careless Love

2. Sorrow, sorrow, to my heart,
   Sorrow, sorrow, to my heart,
   Sorrow, sorrow, to my heart,
   When me and my true love must part.

3. Oh, it's broke this heart of mine,
   Oh, it's broke this heart of mine,
   Oh, it's broke this heart of mine,
   It'll break that heart of yours sometime.

Cindy

I wish I had a needle
As fine as I could sew,
I'd sew the girls to my coat tail
And down the road I'd go.

Cindy in the springtime,
Cindy in the fall,
If I can't have my Cindy,
I'll have no girl at all. Chorus:

Poor Wayfaring Stranger

Buffalo Gals

Bright, walking tempo

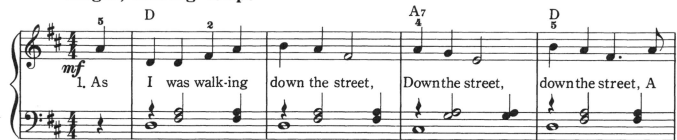

Chorus

2. I asked her if she'd stop and talk,

   Stop and talk, stop and talk,

   Her feet covered up the whole sidewalk,

   She was fair to view.

   Chorus :

3. I asked her if she'd be my wife,

   Be my wife, be my wife,

   Then I'd be happy all my life,

   If she'd marry me.

   Chorus :

Git Along Little Doggies
(Whoopee ti yi yo)

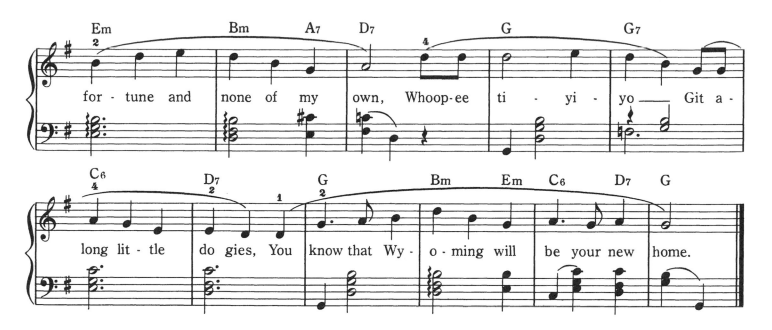

for - tune and none of my own, Whoop-ee ti - yi - yo — Git a-

long lit - tle do gies, You know that Wy - o - ming will be your new home.

The Riddle Song
(I Gave My Love A Cherry)

Freely moving

I gave my love a cher - ry that has no stones, I gave my love a chick-en that has no bones, I gave my love a ring— that has no end, I gave my love a ba - by that's no cry - in'.

2. How can there be a cherry that has no stone,
How can there be a chicken that has no bone,
How can there be a ring that has no end,
How can there be a baby with no cryin'?

3. A cherry when it's blooming, it has no stone,
A chicken when it's pipping, it has no bone,
A ring when it's rolling, it has no end,
A baby when it's sleeping, there's no cryin'.

Green Grow The Lilacs

Moderately

Green grow the li-lacs all spark-ling with dew. I'm

lone-ly, my dar-ling, since part-ing with you. But

by our next meet-ing I hope to prove true, And

change the green li-lacs to the red, white, and blue.

2. I had a sweetheart, but now I have none,
   Since she's gone and left me, I care
      not for one.
   Since she's gone and left me, contented
      I'll be,
   For she loves another one better than me.

3. I wrote love letters in rosy red lines,
   She sent me an answer all twisted in twines,
   Saying, "Keep your love letters and I
      will keep mine,
   Just you write to your love and I'll
      write to mine."

Shenandoah

2. O Shenandoah, I love your daughter,
Way hay, my rolling river!
She lives across the stormy water,
Way hay, I'm bound away,
'Cross the wide Missouri.

3. Oh Shenandoah, I'm bound to leave you,
Way hay, my rolling river!
Oh, Shenandoah, I'll not deceive you,
Way hay, I'm bound away,
'Cross the wide Missouri.

All The Pretty Little Horses

Slowly, tenderly

Hush - a - by, Don't you cry, Go to slee-py, lit - tle ba - by.

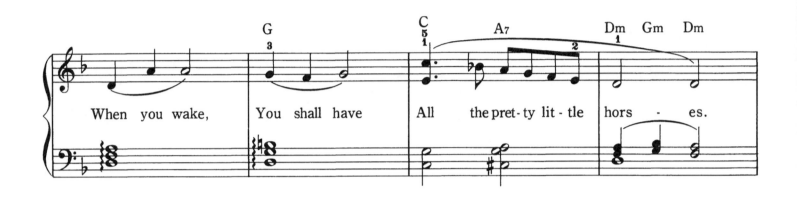

When you wake, You shall have All the pret-ty lit - tle hors - es.

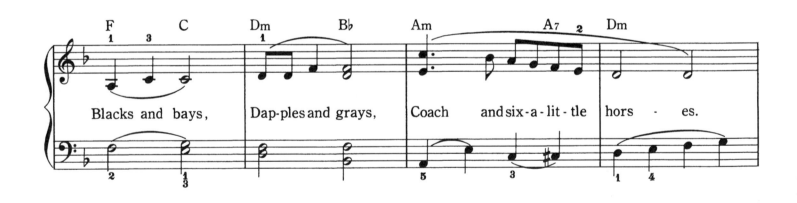

Blacks and bays, Dap-ples and grays, Coach and six - a - lit - tle hors - es.

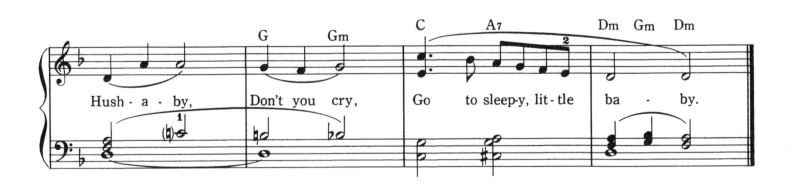

Hush - a - by, Don't you cry, Go to sleep-y, lit - tle ba - by.

Blow Ye Winds In The Morning

2. They tell you of the clipper - ships,
   A - going in and out,
   And say you'll take five hundred whales
   Before you're six months out, singing:

   Chorus :

3. It's now we're out to see my boys,
   The wind begins to blow,
   One half of the watch is sick on deck
   And the other half below, singing:

   Chorus :

Goober Peas

On My Journey Home

Slowly, with spirit

1. When I can read my ti - tle clear — to man - sions in the skies, I'll
2. Should earth a - gainst my soul en - gage, — and hell - ish darts be hurled, Then

bid fare - well to ev - 'ry fear — and dry my weep - ing eyes.
I can smile at sa - tan's rage, — and face a frown - ing world. *mf* I

feel like, I feel — like I'm on my jour - ney home, — I

feel like, I feel — like I'm on my jour - ney home.

The Boll Weevil Song

Moderately

1. Oh the boll wee-vil is a lit-tle black bug, Comes from Mex - i - co, they
2. Now the first time I saw that lit-tle black bug, He was set - tin' on the

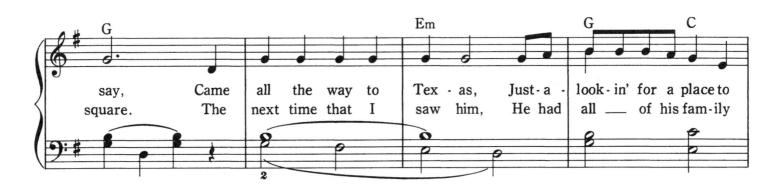

say, Came all the way to Tex - as, Just-a-look-in' for a place to
square. The next time that I saw him, He had all ___ of his fam-ily

stay, Just a look-in'for a home, ___ Just a lookin'for a home! ___
there,

3. So the farmer he went and took the
   boll weevil,
   And he put him in hot sand.
   The weevil yelled - it's darn hot,
   But I'll stand it like a man,
   'Cause we gotta have a home,
   'Cause we gotta have a home!

4. And the farmer he had no cotton to
   sell,
   He said: I'm in a fix,
   That weevil ate my cotton,
   And left me only sticks,
   Now I'm gonna lose my home,
   Now I'm gonna lose my home!

Nine Hundred Miles

Moderately

I am rid-ing on this train, There are tears in my eyes,

Try'n' to read a let-ter from my home. ___ If this train runs me

right, I'll be home to-mor-row night, For I'm nine - hun-dred miles_ from my

home, ___ And I hate to hear that lone-some whis-tle blow. ___

2. Well this train I ride on is a hundred coaches long,

   You can head the whistle blow a hundred miles;

   If this train runs me right, I'll be home tomorrow night,

   For I'm nine hundred miles from my home,

   And I hate to hear that lonesome whistle blow.

Peter Gray

3. Just as they were about to wed
   Her father did say no,
   And consequently she was sent
   Beyond the Ohio.   Chorus:

4. When Peter heard his love was lost,
   He knew not what to say,
   He'd half a mind to jump into
   The Susquehan-ni-a.   Chorus:

5. Now Peter went away out west
   For furs and other skins,
   But he was caught and scalp-i-ed
   By bloody Indians.   Chorus:

6. When Lucy Annie heard the news,
   She straightway took to bed,
   And never did get up again
   Until she di-i-ed.   Chorus:

Go 'Way From My Window

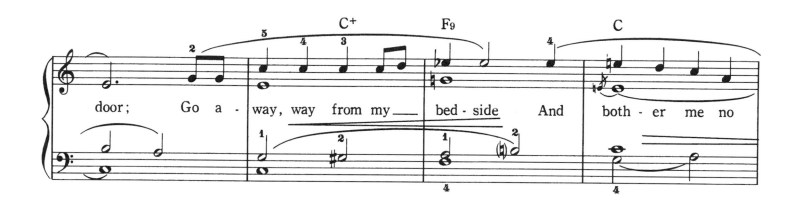

2. Please go and tell my brothers,

   Tell all my sisters too,

   That the reason that my heart is broke

   Is all because of you,

   Is all because of you.

3. Go away from my window,

   Go away from my door,

   Go away, way from my bedside

   And bother me no more,

   And bother me no more.

Old Joe Clark

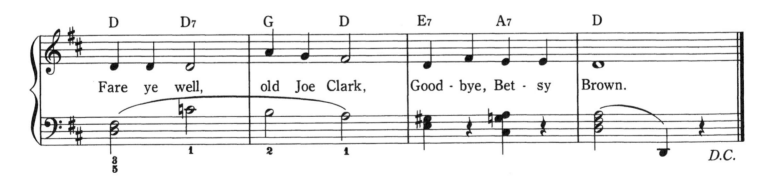

3. When I was a little boy,

I used to want a knife;

Now I am a bigger boy,

I only want a wife.

Chorus:

4. I wish I had a sweetheart;

I'd set her on the shelf,

And ev'ry time she'd smile at me

I'd get up there myself.

Chorus:

Hush, Little Baby

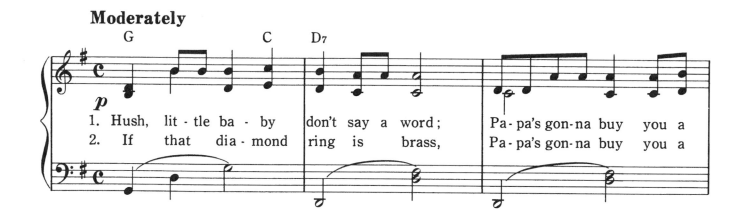

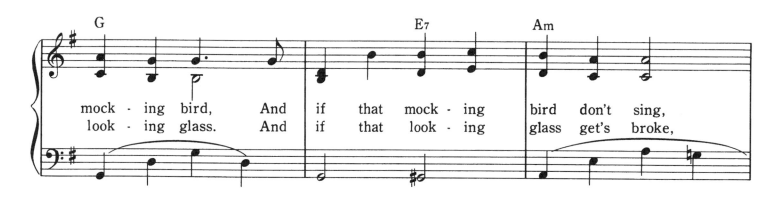

3. And if that billy goat don't pull,

Papa's gonna buy you a cart and bull.

And if that cart and bull turn over,

Papa's gonna buy you a dog named Rover.

4. And if that dog named Rover don't bark,

Papa's gonna buy you a horse and cart.

And if that horse and cart fall down,

You'll still be the sweetest little baby in town.

This Train

2. This train don't carry no gamblers, This train,
This train don't carry no gamblers, This train,
This train don't carry no gamblers,
No hypocrites, no midnight ramblers,
This train is bound for glory, This train.

3. This train don't carry no liars, This train,
This train don't carry no liars, This train,
This train don't carry no liars,
The truth is what the Lord desires,
This train is bound for glory, This train.

Down In The Valley

2. Roses love sunshine, violets love dew;
   Angels in Heaven know I love you.
   Know I love you, dear, know I love you;
   Angels in Heaven know I love you.

3. Writing this letter, containing three lines,
   Answer my question, "Will you be mine?"
   Will you be mine, dear, will you be mine?
   Answer my question, "Will you be mine?"

The Crawdad Song

Lively

You get a line and I'll get a pole — hon-ey,

You get a line and I'll get a pole — babe —

You get a line and I'll get a pole, and we'll go down to the craw-dad hole, —

hon-ey, su-gar ba-by mine. —

2. Yonder comes a man with a sack on his back, honey,

Yonder comes a man with a sack on his back, babe,

Yonder comes a man with a sack on his back,

Packin' all crawdads he can pack,

Honey, sugar-baby mine.

3. I heard the duck say to the drake, honey,

I heard the duck say to the drake, honey,

I heard the duck say to the drake,

There ain't no crawdads in this lake,

Honey, sugar-baby mine.

Come All Ye Fair And Tender Ladies

Moderately

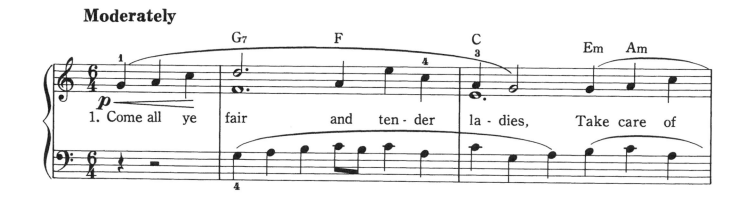

1. Come all ye fair and ten - der la - dies, Take care of

how you court young men. They're like the stars on a sum - mer

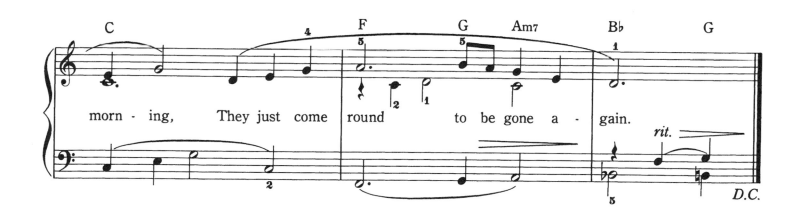

morn - ing, They just come round to be gone a - gain.

rit.

D.C.

2. Come all ye fair and tender ladies,

When they declare their love is true

Straightway they'll go for to court another,

And where, oh where, is the love for you?

Were You There?

Rather slow, with deep feeling

2. Were you there, when they nailed him to the tree?
   Were you there, when they nailed him to the tree?
   Oh____ sometimes, it causes me to tremble,
   tremble, tremble,
   Were you there, when they nailed him to the tree?

3. Were you there, when the sun refused to shine?
   Were you there, when the sun refused to shine?
   Oh____ sometimes, it causes me to tremble,
   tremble, tremble,
   Were you there, when the sun refused to shine?

O Charlie Is My Darling

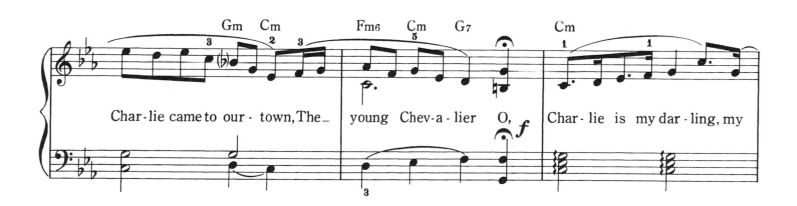

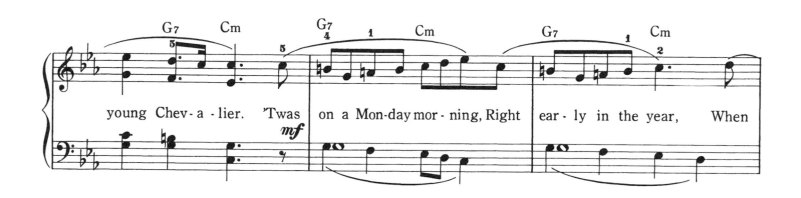

The State Of El-a-noy

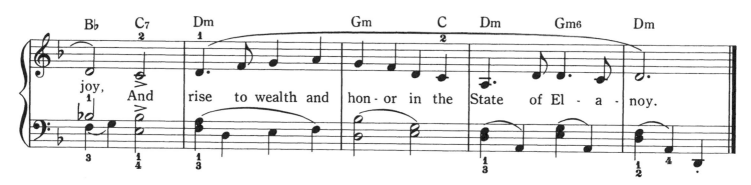

'Twas here came Queen of Sheba with Solomon of old,

With donkey loads of spices, pomegranates and gold;

And when she saw this lovely land her heart was filled with joy;

Straightway she said, "I'd like to be a queen in El-a-noy.

Chorus:

Paper Of Pins

Moderately

He: I'll give to you the keys to my chest

That you may have gold at your request;

If you will marry me, me, me,

If you will marry me.

She: Oh, I'll accept the keys to your chest

That I may have gold at my request;

And I will marry you, you, you,

And I will marry you.

He: Oh, you love coffee and you love tea,

You love gold, but you don't love me;

So I'll not marry you, you, you,

So I'll not marry you.

The Cowboy's Lament
(The Streets of Laredo)

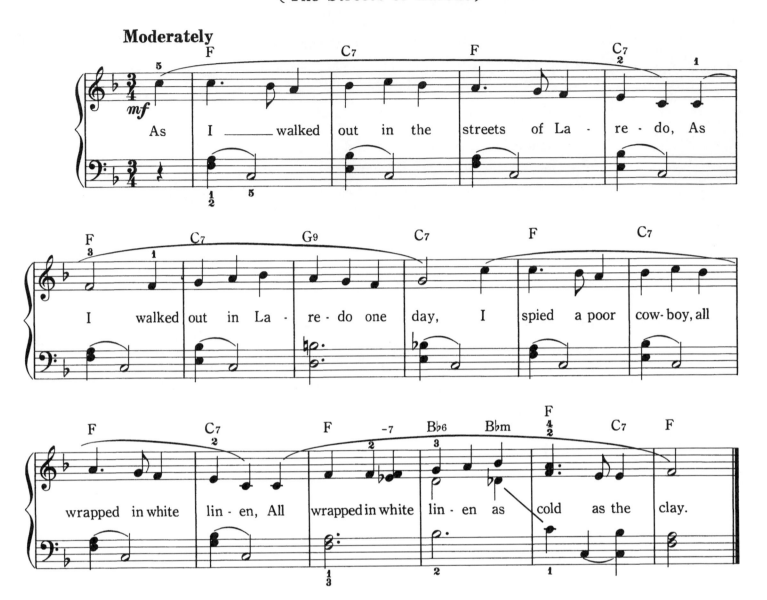

Moderately

As I ___ walked out in the streets of La - re - do, As I walked out in La - re - do one day, I spied a poor cow-boy, all wrapped in white lin - en, All wrapped in white lin - en as cold as the clay.

2. "I see by your outfit that you are a cowboy,"
   These words he did say as I clamly went by.
   "Come sit down beside me and hear my sad story,
   I'm shot in the breast and I know I must die."

3. "It was once in the saddle I used to go dashing,
   Once in the saddle I gallop'd away,
   First down to the barroom and then to the card house,
   Shot in the breast, and I'm dying to-day."

4. "Get six of my buddies to carry my coffin,
   Six pretty maidens to sing a sad song,
   Take me to the valley and lay the sod o'er me,
   For I'm a young cowboy who knows he did wrong."

5. "Go fetch me a cup, a cup of cold water,
   To cool my parched lips," the cowboy then said,
   Before I returned, the spirit had left him,
   And gone to its Maker, the cowboy was dead.

The Bird Song

2. "Hi!" said the little leather-winged bat,
   "I will tell you the reason that,
   The reason that I fly in the night
   Is because I've lost my heart's delight."
   Chorus:

3. "Hi!" said the woodpecker, sitting on a fence,
   "Once I courted a handsome wench,
   She got sulky and from me fled,
   And ever since then my head's been red."
   Chorus:

Who Will Shoe Your Pretty Little Foot

Look Down That Lonesome Road

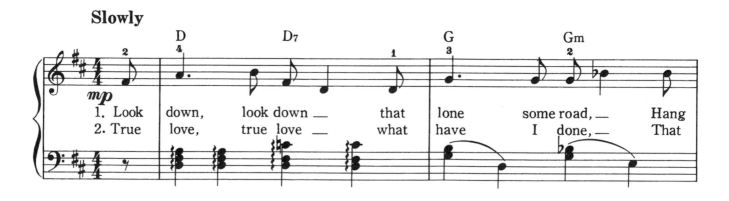

down your head and sigh. The best of friends must
you should treat me so? You caused me to walk — and

part some day, — And why not you and I.
talk with you, — Like I ne'er done be - fore.

Every Night The Sun Goes In

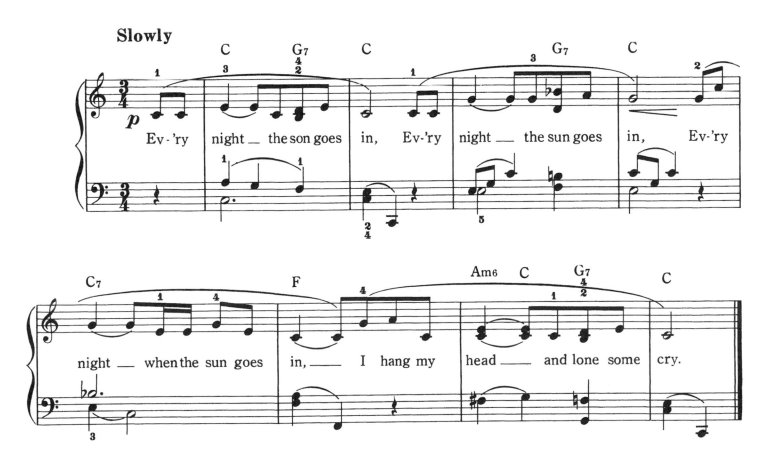

Slowly

Ev-'ry night — the son goes in, Ev-'ry night — the sun goes in, Ev-'ry

night — when the sun goes in, — I hang my head — and lone some cry.

Three Fiddle Tunes

1. Turkey In The Straw

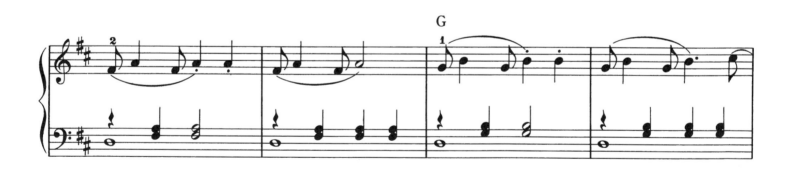

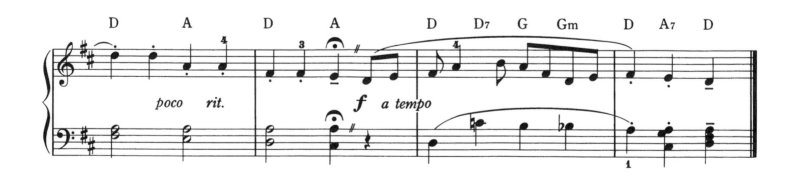

2. Arkansas Traveler

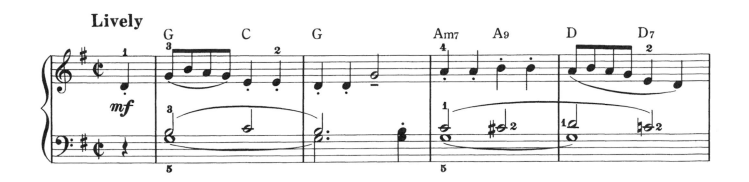

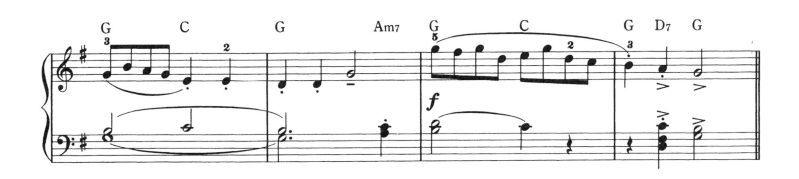

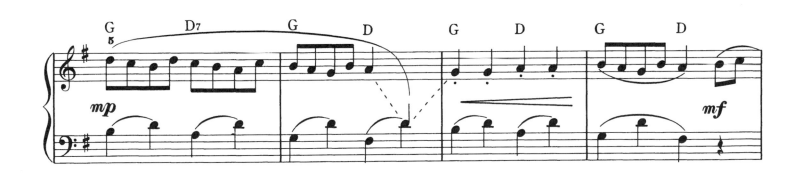

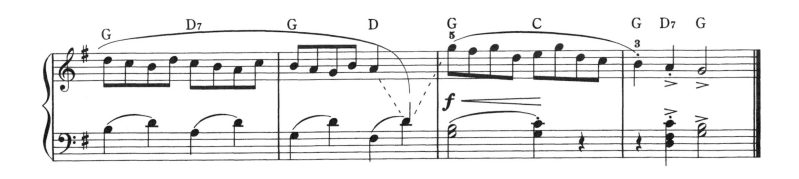

46

3. McLeod's Reel

Greensleeves

Acres Of Clams

Moderately lively

1. I've wan-dered all o-ver this coun-try, Pros-pect-ing and dig-ging for gold. I've tun-nel'd, hy-drau-licked and cra-dled, And I near-ly froze in the cold.

Chorus And so I de-part-ed for Pu-get Sound, A-way from a world full of shams, I sing of my hap-py con-

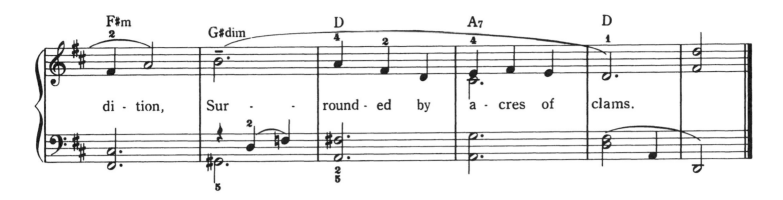

2. For one who got wealthy by mining,
   I saw many hundreds get poor.
   I made up my mind to go digging
   For something a little more sure.

   Chorus:

3. No longer the slave of ambition,
   No leader, just one of the lambs,
   I sing of my happy condition,
   Surrounded by acres of clams.

   Chorus:

I Know Where I'm Goin'

2. I have stockings of silk,
   Shoes of fine green leather,
   Combs to buckle my hair,
   And a ring for every finger.

3. Feather beds are soft,
   And painted rooms are bonny,
   But I would leave them all
   For my handsome, winsome Johnny.

Molly Malone
(Cockles and Mussels)

2. She was a fishmonger, but sure 'twas no wonder,
   For so were her father and mother before,
   And they each pushed their wheel-barrow
   Through streets broad and narrow
   Crying: "Cockles and mussels alive, alive, oh!"
      Chorus:

3. She died of a "faver," and no one could save her,
   And that was the end of sweet Molly Malone;
   Her ghost wheels her barrow
   Through streets broad and narrow
   Crying: "Cockles and mussels alive, alive, oh!"
      Chorus:

A - Roving

2. I took the maiden for a walk,

   Mark well what I do say!

   I took the maiden for a walk

   And sweet and loving was our talk,

   And I'll go no more a-roving

   With you, fair maid!

   Chorus:

3. I put my arm around her waist,

   Mark well what I do say!

   I put my arm around her waist,

   She said, "Young man, you're in great haste."

   And I'll go no more a-roving

   With you, fair maid!

   Chorus:

Home On The Range

an - te - lope play, _____ Where sel - dom is heard a dis-

cour - a - ging word, And the skies are not clou - dy all day. _____

Pick A Bale Of Cotton

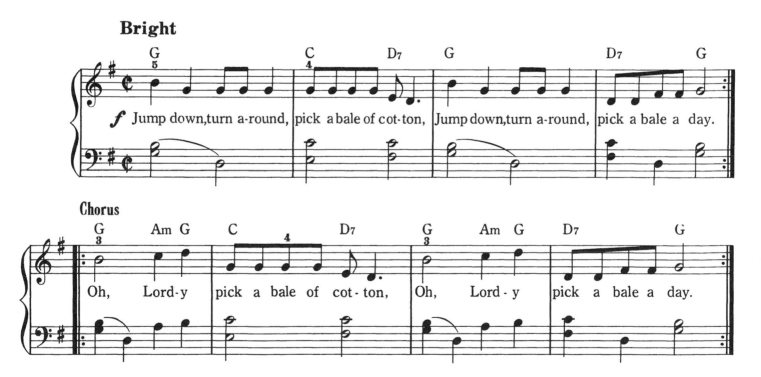

Bright

Jump down, turn a-round, pick a bale of cot-ton, Jump down, turn a-round, pick a bale a day.

Chorus

Oh, Lord-y pick a bale of cot-ton, Oh, Lord-y pick a bale a day.

2. Me and my gal can pick a bale of cotton,
   Me and my gal can pick a bale a day.

   Chorus:

3. Me and my friend can pick a bale of cotton,
   Me and my friend can pick a bale a day.

   Chorus:

Nobody Knows The Trouble I've Seen

Joshua Fit The Battle Of Jericho

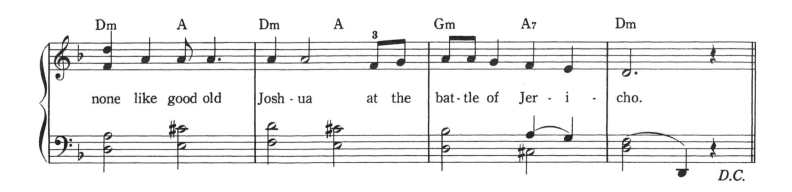

The Big Rock Candy Mountain

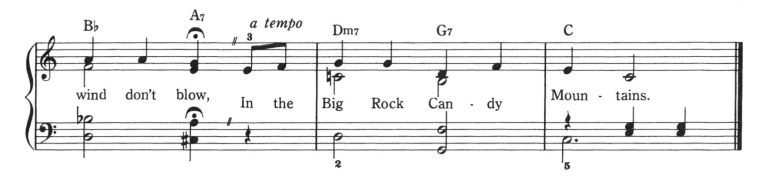

2. In the Big Rock Candy Mountains
   You never change your socks,
   And little streams of alkyhol
   Come tricklin' down the rocks.
   The shacks all have to tip their hats
   And the railrood bulls are blind,
   There's a lake of stew and of whiskey too,
   And you paddle all around in a big canoe,
   In the Big Rock Candy Mountains.

3. In the Big Rock Candy Mountains
   The jails are made of tin,
   And you can bust right out again
   As soon as they put you in.
   There ain't no short handles shovels,
   No axes, saws, or picks,
   I'm a-goin' to stay where you sleep all day,
   Where they boiled in oil the inventor of toil,
   In the Big Rock Candy Mountains.

O Whistle And I'll Come To You

Rather freely

I Know My Love

The Wraggle-Taggle Gypsies

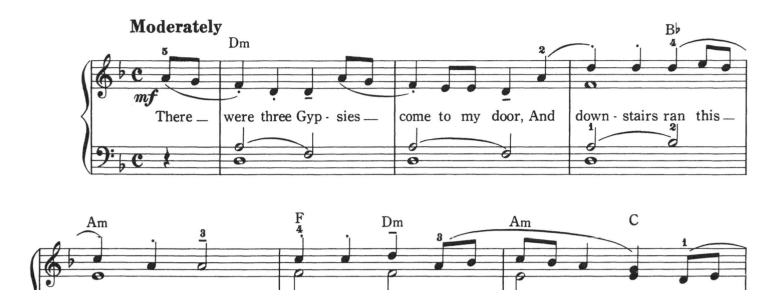

2. Then she pulled off her silk finished gown,

   And put on hose of leather, O!

   The ragged rags about our door,

   She's gone with the wraggle-taggle gypsies O!

3. Last night she slept on a goose feather bed,

   A home so warm had my lady O.

   Now I'm told she is hungry and cold,

   Far away with the wraggle-taggle gypsies O!

Drill Ye Tarriers Drill

With vigorous motion

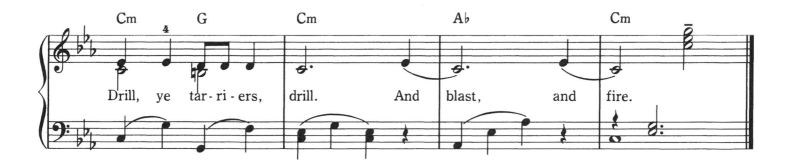

Drill, ye tar-ri-ers, drill. And blast, and fire.

2. Now our foreman was Jean McCann,

By God, he was a blame mean man;

Past week a premature blast went off,

And a mile in the air went big Jim Goff.

Chorus:

3. Next time pay day comes around,

Jim Goff a dollar short was found;

When asked, "What for?" came this reply:

"You're docked for the time you was up in the

sky.   Chorus:

Cripple Creek

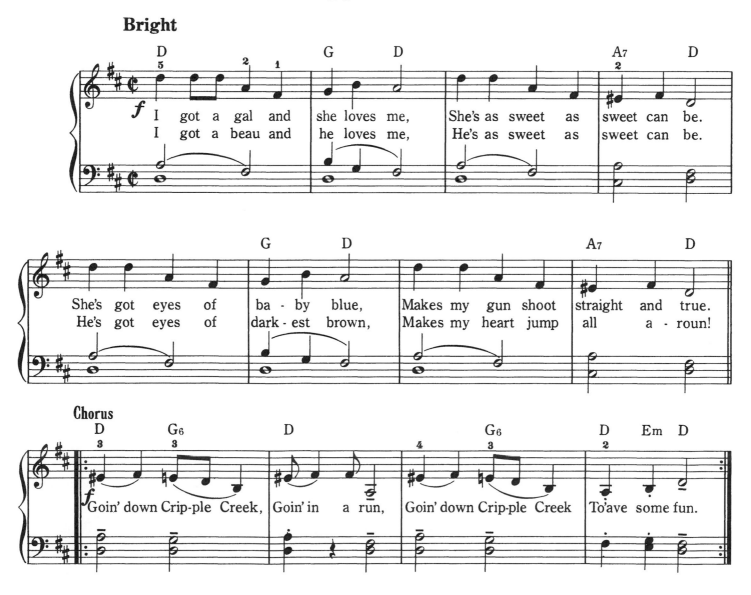

Bright

I got a gal and she loves me, She's as sweet as sweet can be.
I got a beau and he loves me, He's as sweet as sweet can be.

She's got eyes of ba - by blue, Makes my gun shoot straight and true.
He's got eyes of dark - est brown, Makes my heart jump all a - roun!

Chorus

Goin' down Crip-ple Creek, Goin' in a run, Goin' down Crip-ple Creek To 'ave some fun.

Go Down Moses

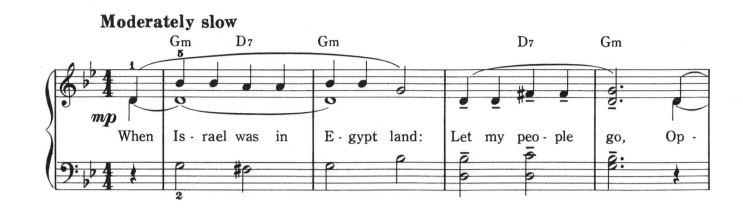

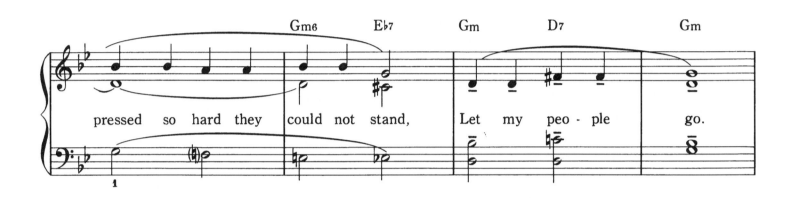

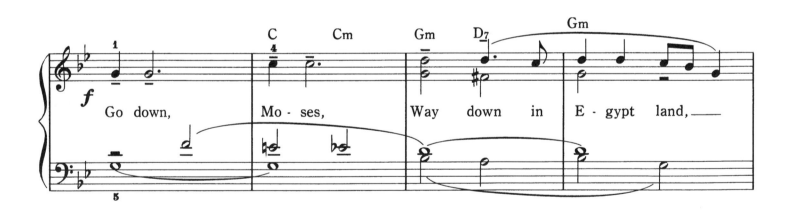

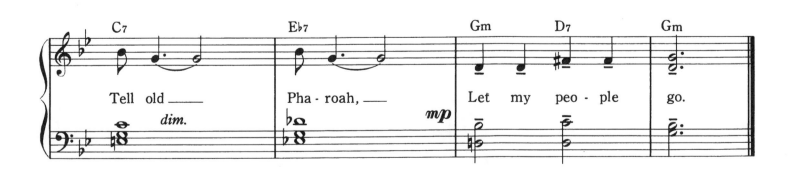

I Was Born About Ten Thousand Years Ago

3. I saw Jonah when he shoved off in the whale,
   And I thought he'd never live to tell the tale,
   But old Jonah'd eaten garlic, and he gave the whale the colic,
   So he coughed him up and let him outta jail.

4. I saw Samson when he laid the village cold,
   I saw Daniel tame the lions in their hold;
   I helped build the tower of Babel up as high as they were able,
   And there's lots of other things I haven't told.

Prayer Of Thanksgiving

Wilt Heden Nu Treden

Dutch

My One And Only Love

Csak Egy Kislány

Tiritomba

Lively

Italian

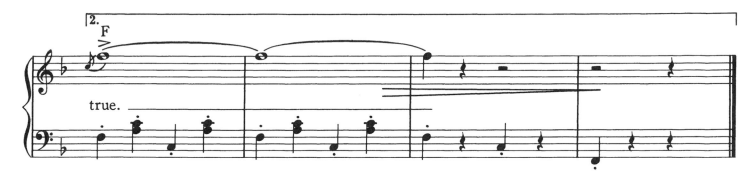

Sera jette, sera jette a la marina,

Pe travà 'na 'nnamorata,

Janca e rossa, janca e rossa aggrazziata,

Fatto proprio pe scialà.

Refrain: Tiritomba, tiritomba,

Tiritomba, n'e lu vero si ono?

Tiritomba, tiritomba,

Tiritomba all 'arià và!

Finnish Polka
Halihilja

Swiss Yodel Song

Lively walking tempo

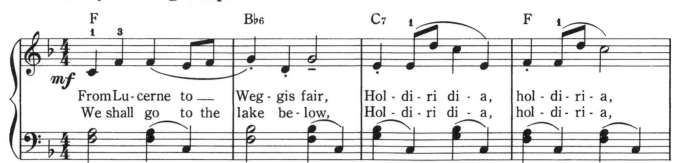

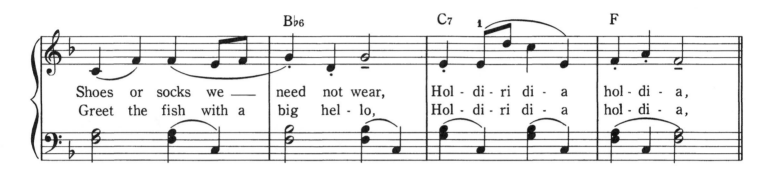

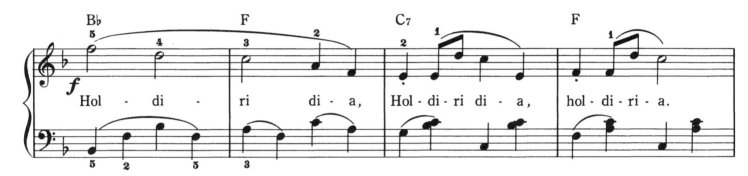

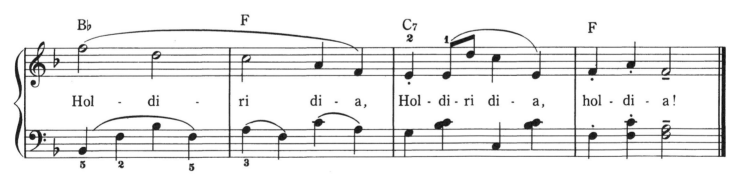

Vo Luzern uf Weggis zue,
Holdiri dia, holdiria;
Bruuch me weder Strumpf no Schue,
Holdiri dia, holdia. Refrain:

Me cha fahren ufem See,
Holdiri dia, holdiria;
Un die schone Fischli g'seh,
Holdiri dia, holdia. Refrain:

Per Spelmann

Norwegian

Per Spelmann han hadde ei einaste ku;
Per Spelmann han hadde ei einaste ku.
Han bytte bort kua, fekk fela igjen,
Han bytte bort kua, fekk fela igjen.
Du gamle, gode fiolin, du fiolin,
Du fela mi.

Per Spelmann han spela, og fela ho let,
Per Spelmann han spela, og fela ho let.
Sa gutane dansa, og gjentene gret,
Sa gutane dansa, og gjentene gret.
Du gamle, gode fiolin, du fiolin,
Du fela mi.

La Belle Rose

French - Canadian

Moderately

2. ‖: Je l'ai porté chez mon père, :‖
Entre Paris et Rouen,
La belle rose,
Entre Paris et Rouen,
La belle ros' du rosier blanc.

3. ‖: Je n'ai pas trouvé personne :‖
Que le rossignol chantant,
La belle rose,
Que le rossignol chantant,
La belle ros' du rosier blanc.

4. ‖: Qui me dit dans son langage :‖
"Mari - toi, car il est temps,"
La belle rose,
Mari - toi, car il est temps,
La belle ros' du rosier blanc.

5. ‖: "Comment veux - tu que j'm'y marie? :‖
Mon père en est pas content."
La belle rose,
Mon pere en est pas content,
La belle ros' du rosier blanc.

New Year's Song

Saint Basil

2. Vasta ia penna ke harti

   Zaharokantió zimoti

   Harti, harti ke kalamari

   Thes eme, thes eme to palikari.

3. To kalamari eghrafe,

   Ti mira too tin eleghe

   Ke to, ke to harti omili

   To hriso, to hriso mas karghiófili.

4. Arhiminiá kiárhiminiá

   Psili mou thendrolivaniá,

   Kiárhi, kiárhi kalos mas hronos

   Eklisiá, eklisiá me taghió thronos

5. Arhi pou vghiken o Christos

   Aghios ke Pnevmatikos

   Sti ghi, sti ghi na perpatisi

   Ke na mas, ke na mas kalokarthisi.

Vermeland

English words by
Sylvia Eversole

Swedish

Moderately slow

Oh, Ver - me - land, my home land, your beau - ty fills my heart, I
sing your prais - es o - ver land and o - cean. Where-
ev - er I have wan - dered, no place in all the world Has
stirred with - in my heart this fond de - vo - tion. Where
might - y hills and splen - did for - ests rise to meet the sky, Where

Ack, Vär - me - land, du skö - na, du här - li - ga du
kro - na bland Sve - a - ri - kes län - der!
Och kom - me jag än midt i det för - lof - va - de land,
till värm - land jag än - då å - ter - vän - der. Ja,
där vill jag lef - va, ja, där - vill jag dö: Och

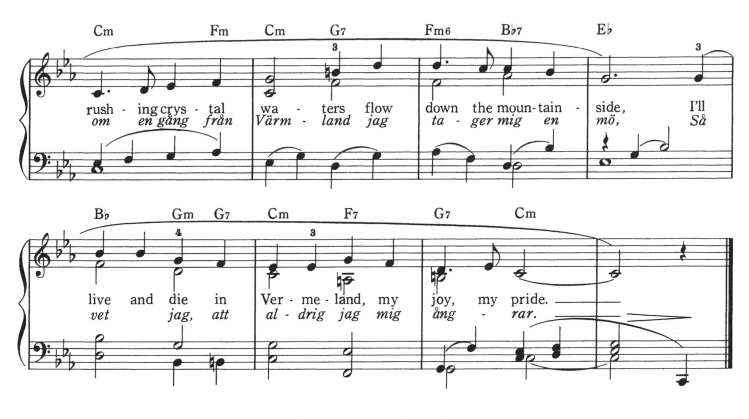

rush - ing crys - tal | wa - ters flow | down the moun - tain - side, | I'll
om en gång från | *Värm - land jag* | *ta - ger mig en mö,* | *Så*

live and die in | Ver - me - land, my | joy, my pride. |
vet jag, att | *al - drig jag mig* | *ång - rar.*

Stenka Razin

English words by
Sylvia Eversole

Moderately

Russian

1. Once a | might - y kos - sack | he - ro Took a | prin - cess for his
Iz za | *os - trah - va, na* | *streh - zhen, Na prah -* | *stor rech - noy vahl -*

bride, and he | sailed the riv - er | Vol - ga, With his | sweet - heart by his | side.
ny, | *Vi - pli - va - li ras - pis -* | *ny - ye Ah - strah -* | *groo - dy - yeh chel -* | *ny.*

2. Stenka Razin, cried his comrades
   You have lost your fighting heart,
   Love has weakened all your courage,
   You are from us set apart.

3. At these words, so harsh and taunting,
   Stenka Razin, strong and brave,
   Threw his bride, his lovely princess
   In the Volga's foaming rave.

(Repeat 1st verse pp)

Auprès De Ma Blonde

Comfortably, with a lilt

French

Dans le jar-din d'mon pè - re les li - las sont fleu - ris, ____ Dans
La caille, la tour-te-rel - le, et la jo-lie per - drix, ____ La

le jar-din d'mon pè - re les li - las sont fleu - ris. ____ Tous
caille, la tour-te-rel - le, et la jo-lie per - drix, ____ Et

les oi-seaux du mon - de y vien - nent faire leur nid.
ma jo-lie co - lom - be qui chante jour et nu - it.

Refrain

Au - près de ma blon - de Qu'il fait bon, fait bon, fait bon,

Au - près de ma blon - de Qu'il fait bon dor - mir! ____

Slovakian Dance Tune

Tancuj, Vykrúcaj

English words by
Sylvia Eversole

Lively

Gyp - sies playing bright - ly and clear - ly, So choose a
Tan - cuj, tan - cuj, vy - krú - caj, vy - krú - caj, Len mi

part - ner that you love dear - ly, Step out and join the
pie - cku ně - srú - caj, ně - sru - caj; Lep - šie pie - cka

swing - ing and sway - ing, We'll dance un - til the mu - sic stops play - ing.
na zi - mu, na zi - mu, Ně - ma kaž - dý pe - ri - nu, pe - ri - nu.

Tra - la - la - la - la, Tra - la - la - la - la, Tra - la -

la - la, Tra - la - la - la, la - la - la - la! Tra - la - la - la - la!

Tum - Balalaika

Israeli

Shteht a bocher und er tracht,
Tracht und tracht die ganze Nacht;
Vemen zu nehmen und nit farshemen,
Vemen zu nehmen un nit farshemen.
Refrain:

Medel, medel, 'chvell ba dir fregen,
Vos ken vaksen, vaksen on regen,
Vos ken brennen on nit oifheren
Vos ken benken, vehnen on trerren
Refrain:

Narishe Bocher vos darfst du fregen
A stehn ken vaksen, vaksen on regen;
Liebe ken brennen on nit oifheren,
A hartz ken benken, vehnen on trennen.
Refrain:

Grün, Grün, Grün

German

Weiss, weiss, weiss sind alle meine Kleider,

Weiss, weiss, weiss liebt jederman.

Darum lieb' ich alles was so weiss ist,

Denn mein Lieb ein Backer ist.

Schwarz, schwarz schwarz sind alle meine Kleider,

Schwarz, schwarz, schwarz liebt jederman.

Darum lieb' ich alles was so schwarz ist,

Denn mein Lieb ein Schornsteinfeger ist.

Cherry Blossoms
Sakura

With slow, delicate motion

Japanese

Cher - ry trees bloom - ing bright, Cher - ry blos - soms are in sight,
Sa - ku - ra *Sa - ku - ra* *Ya - yo - i no* *So - ra - wa*

Love - ly flow - ers pink and white. They're like sil - ver mist in the air,
Mi - wa - ta - su *ka - gi - ri* *Ka - su - mi ka* *ku - mo - ka*

They're like float - ing clouds ev - 'ry - where. Come with me,
Ni - o - i zo *i - zu - ru* *I - za - ya*

Come to see Blos - soms on the cher - ry tree. Come with me,
I - za - ya *Mi ni yu - ka - un.*

Mother Dear

Matuś Moja, Matuś

English words by
Sylvia Eversole

Polish

1. Matuś moja, matuś wydaj mnie za Jasia,
   spobodały mi sie koleczka u pasa, oj dana.
   Oj dana, oj dana, etc.

2. Koleczka u pasa, buciki czewone,
   o mój miły Jasiu, pojmij mnie za żonę, oj dana.
   Oj dana, oj dana, etc.

3. Danaż moj dana, nie pójdę za pana,
   jeno za takiego, jako i ja sama, oj dana.
   Oj dana, oj dana, etc.

4. Bo panu potrzeba puchowych poduszek,
   a ja chlopcu ze wsi podścielę fartuszek, oj dana.
   Oj dana, oj dana, etc.

The Little Deer
El Venadito

Mexican

Rather lively

I am like a lit-tle deer, I'm liv-ing high up on the moun-tain
Soy un po-bre ve-na-di-to que ha-bi-ta en la se-rra-ni - a!

I'm so shy, du-ring the day I keep a-way from ev-'ry
Soy un po-bre ve-na-di-to que ha-bi-ta en la se-rra-

foun-tain; But at night I have no fear, I go to
ni - a! Co-mo no soy tan man-si-to no ba-

see my lit-tle "deer," And whis-per man-y, man-y ten-der songs of love in-to her
jo al 'a-gua de di - a; de no-che, po-co a po-qui-to, yen tus bra-zos, vi-da

ear. But at
mi - a. Co-mo